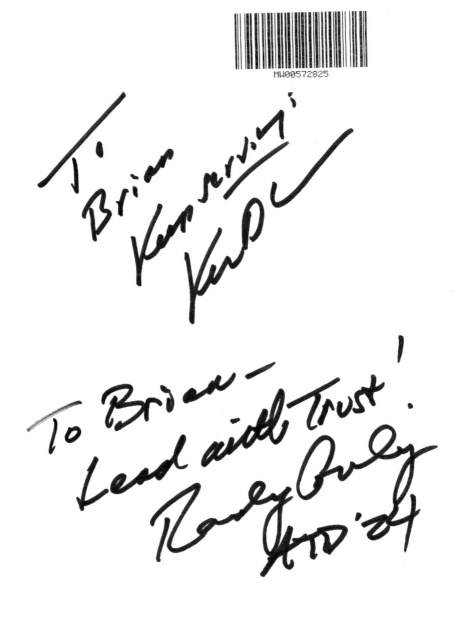

To Brian
Keep serving!
Ken D

To Brian —
Lead with Trust!
Randy Conley
HTT '24

Simple
Truths *of*
Leadership
Playbook

Simple
Truths *of*
Leadership
Playbook

**A 52-Week Game Plan for Becoming
a TRUSTED SERVANT LEADER**

Ken Blanchard
Randy Conley
WITH RENEE BROADWELL

Berrett–Koehler Publishers, Inc.

The One Minute Manager® and SLII® are registered trademarks of Blanchard®.

Berrett-Koehler Publishers, Inc.
1333 Broadway, Suite 1000
Oakland, CA 94612-1921
Tel: (510) 817-2277
Fax: (510) 817-2278
www.bkconnection.com

ORDERING INFORMATION
Quantity sales. Special discounts are available on quantity purchases by corporations,
associations, and others. For details, contact the "Special Sales Department" at the Berrett-
Koehler address above.
Individual sales. Berrett-Koehler publications are available through most bookstores. They
can also be ordered directly from Berrett-Koehler: Tel: (800) 929-2929; Fax: (802) 864-7626;
www.bkconnection.com.
Orders for college textbook / course adoption use. Please contact Berrett-Koehler: Tel: (800)
929-2929; Fax: (802) 864-7626.

Distributed to the U.S. trade and internationally by Penguin Random House Publisher
Services.

Berrett-Koehler and the BK logo are registered trademarks of Berrett-Koehler Publishers, Inc.

Printed in the United States of America

Berrett-Koehler books are printed on long-lasting acid-free paper. When it is available, we
choose paper that has been manufactured by environmentally responsible processes. These
may include using trees grown in sustainable forests, incorporating recycled paper, minimiz-
ing chlorine in bleaching, or recycling the energy produced at the paper mill.

Library of Congress Cataloging-in-Publication Data

Names: Blanchard, Kenneth H., author. | Conley, Randy, author. | Broadwell,
    Renee, author.
Title: Simple truths of leadership playbook : a 52-week game plan for
    becoming a trusted servant leader / Ken Blanchard, Randy Conley, with
    Renee Broadwell.
Description: Oakland, CA : Berrett-Koehler Publishers, [2024] | Includes
    bibliographical references and index.
Identifiers: LCCN 2023022885 (print) | LCCN 2023022886 (ebook) |
    ISBN 9781523006113 (hardcover ; alk. paper) | ISBN 9781523006120 (pdf) |
    ISBN 9781523006137 (epub)
Subjects: LCSH: Leadership. | Servant leadership. | Trust.
Classification: LCC HD57.7 .B56333 2023 (print) | LCC HD57.7 (ebook) |
    DDC 658.4/092—dc23/eng/20230512
LC record available at https://lccn.loc.gov/2023022885
LC ebook record available at https://lccn.loc.gov/2023022886

First Edition
30 29 28 27 26 25 24 23   10 9 8 7 6 5 4 3 2 1

Book production: PeopleSpeak
Cover design: Irene Morris with Adrian Morgan

Contents

Introduction: Dear Trusted Servant Leader   1

PART ONE: SERVANT LEADERSHIP

1. Servant leadership is the best way to achieve both great results and great relationships.   4

2. Every great organization has a compelling vision.   6

3. Servant leaders turn the traditional pyramid upside down.   8

4. All good performance starts with clear goals.   10

5. The key to developing people is to catch them doing something right.   12

6. Praise progress!   14

7. When people are off track, don't reprimand them—redirect them.   16

8. The best minute servant leaders spend is the one they invest in people.   18

9. Effective servant leaders realize they have to use different strokes for different folks.   20

10. Effective servant leaders don't just use different strokes for *different* folks, they also use different strokes for the *same* folks. 22

11. Profit is the applause you get for creating a motivating environment for your people so they will take good care of your customers. 24

12. Create autonomy through boundaries. 26

13. You get from people what you expect. 28

14. The best use of power is in service to others. 30

15. Never assume you know what motivates a person. 32

16. People with humility don't think less of themselves, they just think of themselves less. 34

17. It's okay to toot your own horn. 36

18. Don't work harder; work smarter. 38

19. "No one of us is as smart as all of us." —*Eunice Parisi-Carew and Don Carew* 40

20. Love is the answer. What is the question? 42

21. Servant leaders don't command people to obey; they invite people to follow. 44

22. People who plan the battle rarely battle the plan. 46

23. Servant leaders love feedback. 48

Contents

24. People who produce good results feel good about themselves.   50

25. "It's not about you."—*Rick Warren*   52

26. Great leaders SERVE.   54

PART TWO: BUILDING TRUST

27. Leadership begins with trust.   58

28. Building trust is a skill that can be learned and developed.   60

29. "Self-trust is the first secret of success." —*Ralph Waldo Emerson*   62

30. Someone must make the first move to extend trust. Leaders go first.   64

31. "People admire your strengths, but they respect your honesty regarding your vulnerability."—*Colleen Barrett*   66

32. There's no trust without *us*.   68

33. Fear is the enemy of trust.   70

34. A relationship with no trust is like a cell phone with no service or internet—all you can do is play games.   72

35. People don't care how much you know until they know how much you care.   74

36. "People will forget what you said, people will
forget what you did, but people will never forget
how you made them feel."—*Maya Angelou*   76

37. "Your actions speak so loudly I cannot hear
what you are saying."—*Anonymous*   78

38. Tell the truth. Always. It's that simple.   80

39. Don't ever make a promise you can't keep.   82

40. "There's nothing so unequal as the equal
treatment of unequals."—*Anonymous*   84

41. #Trust is always trending. Doing the right
thing never goes out of style.   86

42. True servant leaders admit their mistakes.   88

43. Since we were given two ears and one mouth,
we should listen more than we speak.   90

44. The most important part of leadership is
what happens when you're not there.   92

45. The opposite of trust is not distrust—
it's control.   94

46. People don't resist change; they resist being
controlled.   96

47. People without accurate information cannot
act responsibly, but people with accurate
information are compelled to act responsibly.   98

48. Building trust is a journey, not a destination.   100

49. A successful apology is essential in rebuilding
     trust.   102

50. Apologizing is not necessarily an admission
     of guilt, but it is an admission of responsibility.   104

51. Choosing not to forgive someone is like taking
     poison and waiting for the other person to die.   106

52. Forgiveness is letting go of all hope for a
     better past.   108

Closing Thoughts   111

Resources   113

Works Cited   143

Acknowledgments   145

About the Authors   147

Connect with Blanchard®   149

Join Ken and Randy Online   151

We dedicate this book to our beloved editor and friend
Steve Piersanti, founder of Berrett-Koehler Publishers.
For more than twenty-five years, Steve's positive,
encouraging demeanor and candid guidance
have helped Ken and his coauthors spread the
powerful message of servant leadership.

Thank you, Steve, for everything you do.

Dear Trusted Servant Leader,

Welcome back!

When we wrote *Simple Truths of Leadership: 52 Ways to Be a Servant Leader and Build Trust*, we included a "Making Common Sense Common Practice" section on every page that gave tips on how each Simple Truth could be implemented in the workplace. Our goal was that after reading the book, people would apply those truths to their lives at work and at home. We've been thrilled with the responses from readers telling us about the positive difference the book has made in their leadership journey.

Simple Truths of Leadership Playbook is the next step: a more complete working guide to achieving your goal of becoming a trusted servant leader. We've designed this playbook to be an active deep dive into the 52 Simple Truths of the original book for maximum absorption of these timeless commonsense beliefs about servant leadership and trust. We hope it causes you to thoughtfully reflect on and record your personal leadership philosophies and your performance as a leader.

The playbook focuses on one Simple Truth per week because we believe crafting your approach to leadership is a step-by-step process that takes time. If you read through these pages, do the activities, and apply the lessons to your leadership, at the end of fifty-two weeks you should have the practical skills and experience necessary to be a trusted servant leader.

We believe learning is important—but if you don't take action on what you learn, that information is useless. This may sound strange, but it's true! That's why each Simple Truth ends with a call to action: "Try It This Week." When you put new knowledge into practice, it embeds the information and brings the concepts to life.

Although some areas for writing are available both in the body and at the end of the book, we strongly encourage you to create as much additional physical or digital writing space as you need.

We know you intend to grow in your effectiveness as a trusted servant leader, or you wouldn't have chosen this book. May it help transform your good intentions into powerful results and authentic relationships with the people you serve.

Ken and Randy

PS: Before you begin, be sure to take the Simple Truths of Leadership Self-Assessment, accessible both in the Resources section and by scanning this QR code.

PART ONE

—◦》《◦—

SERVANT
LEADERSHIP

Servant leadership is the best way to achieve both great results and great relationships.

Servant leadership is not an either-or concept. It involves focusing on both results and people. The leadership aspect, which includes vision and direction, is about getting results, while the servant aspect, turning the traditional hierarchical pyramid upside down, is about working with your people and helping them accomplish their goals.

Consider the connection between relationships and results:

- Does your workplace culture seem to be focused more on profits or on people? What prompts you to give that answer? Write about actions top leaders could take to create more of a balance between results and relationships.

  _____

  _____

  _____

  _____

- What kind of attention do you give to relationships? What about results? What could you do better in terms of balancing these?

  _____

  _____

  _____

  _____

TRY IT THIS WEEK

Share this concept with your people and ask them how they see the balance between results and relationships being played out in their work environment. Write about the responses you hear.

(Note: Scan the QR code or go to the Resources section to access the "Are You a Servant Leader but Don't Know It?" assessment.)

—•)}{(•—

SIMPLE TRUTH #2

Every great organization has a compelling vision.

As Jesse Stoner and Ken wrote in their book *Full Steam Ahead!*, a compelling vision has three elements: a significant purpose (what business you are in), a picture of the future (where you are going), and clear values (what will guide your journey). When people support this kind of vision, it creates a culture that drives business results toward the greater good.

As a servant leader, you can start to incorporate these elements into a compelling vision for your organization by responding to these prompts:

- Why is your organization in business? What business would you say you are in?

  _____

  _____

  _____

- If people do their jobs well and your business is successful, what is your company's desired end result? Describe this as a mental image someone could visualize.

  _____

  _____

  _____

- Write about your organization's values and how they are made clear.

  _____

  _____

  _____

TRY IT THIS WEEK

Find out what your company's vision, mission, purpose, and values are. Write about how the organization presents these concepts to people inside and outside the company.

(Note: Scan the QR code or go to the Resources section to access the "Your Personal Compelling Vision" exercise.)

SIMPLE TRUTH #3

Servant leaders turn the traditional pyramid upside down.

O nce an organization's vision and direction are in place, which can involve ideas from others but is primarily the responsibility of leadership, servant leaders turn the traditional pyramid upside down and serve their people by supporting them in achieving their goals and empowering them to live the organization's vision.

Consider the benefits and challenges of being a servant leader:

- Some leaders are concerned that when they start serving and empowering their people, their leadership won't matter as much. Do you agree? Why or why not?

_____

_____

_____

_____

_____

- Would serving team members and helping them win be more or less challenging for a leader than traditional top-down leadership, where the leader calls the shots and leaves people alone to figure out how to meet their goals? Why?

_____

_____

_____

_____

_____

TRY IT THIS WEEK

As a leader, do three things that make servant leadership come alive for your team members. Write about what you do and the reaction you get.

—❧❦—

All good performance starts with clear goals.

*T*he *One Minute Manager*® was a groundbreaking book in 1982 and remained on bestseller lists for years. Why? Because it has three simple secrets for managing: (1) One Minute Goals, (2) One Minute Praisings, and (3) One Minute Re-Directs.

Setting clear goals provides purpose, challenge, and meaning. For a goal to be clear, people need to know what they are being asked to do and what good performance looks like. When a person falls short of achieving a goal, rather than shaming or blaming them, the manager must ask themselves, Did I make their goal clear? If the answer is no, the fault lies with the manager, not the direct report.

Reflect on your own performance:

- In your leadership journey, have you generally been a leader who sets goals, either with or for your direct reports? If not, write about your reasoning.

  _____

  _____

  _____

  _____

- Write about how it would feel to be chastised by your boss for not doing a task correctly if you had never been given specifics on what a good job would look like.

  _____

  _____

  _____

  _____

TRY IT THIS WEEK

What can you do to make sure each of your direct reports is explicitly clear on each of their goals?

—•❯❯❮❮•—

The key to developing people is to catch them doing something right.

Catching people doing something right is the most powerful activity a manager can do. Praising can be done face-to-face, on a video or phone call, or in an email. This simple act builds relationships and self-esteem, rewards positive behavior, and moves people closer to their goals.

To praise effectively, follow these steps: Praise as soon as you know about a person's positive behavior. Tell them what they did right, how you feel about it, and how it helps. Then tell them you know they will keep up the good work.

Reflect on your own previous experiences with praise, or the lack of it, then plan for future praising:

- Write about a time when you accomplished something you were proud of but your boss didn't seem to notice. How did you feel?

  _____

  _____

- Write about a time when you received verbal praise or recognition at a meeting for doing something well. How did you feel then?

  _____

  _____

- Can you think of situations outside the workplace where you could praise someone for doing something right? Write about how giving sincere praise could make someone's day.

  _____

  _____

TRY IT THIS WEEK

Find three situations this week where you catch someone doing something right and praise them. Write about what happens.

—•⋟⋞•—

SIMPLE TRUTH #6

Praise progress!

When a direct report is making headway on a goal or beginning to learn a task, it's important for you as a leader to praise their progress. It lets them know they are on the right track and gives them the confidence they need to keep working toward their goal. If you hold back and wait until they accomplish the goal or complete the task before praising them, the person may lose momentum because you seem to care only about the end result.

Accentuating the positive motivates learners, so praise people when you catch them doing something right as well as when you catch them doing something *approximately* right. Don't wait for perfection—praise progress. It will cheer them on as they move toward their goals.

Consider the pros and cons of praise:

- What's wrong with waiting until people do something exactly right before you praise them?

  _____

  _____

  _____

  _____

  _____

  _____

- Write about the advantages of praising progress.

  _____

  _____

  _____

  _____

  _____

  _____

TRY IT THIS WEEK

Schedule several 1:1 meetings with your people that include progress checks on their task or goal accomplishment. What reactions do you get when you praise them for making progress on a goal?

—⊱⊰—

When people are off track, don't reprimand them—redirect them.

Setting goals and offering praise are ways you can help your people succeed. But what if their progress toward their goals is stalled for some reason? A redirection may be in order.

Use these steps for an effective redirection: Contact the person as soon as you learn of poor performance or behavior. First check that you have made their goal clear. If not, clarify the goal. Discuss the specific problem with them and tell them how you feel. Then let them know you still value them as a contributor.

Consider a leader's role in redirecting poor performance or behavior:

- Write about how negative feedback might become a positive experience.

  _____

  _____

- If a person doesn't understand a goal, why should their manager be held accountable?

  _____

  _____

- As fast as changes happen in the world, people are almost always in a learning mode. Why is this a good reason for redirecting rather than reprimanding?

  _____

  _____

TRY IT THIS WEEK

Write about how you might redirect someone on your team today who is off track. What would you say to help them do better in the future?

SIMPLE TRUTH #8

The best minute servant leaders spend is the one they invest in people.

Many managers don't understand that leadership is not about them—it's about the people they are trying to influence. These kinds of managers don't take the time, even a few minutes a day, to connect with their people. But servant leaders understand that the better they know their team members, the better they will be able to help them achieve their goals.

Spending time with your people builds meaningful connections. It's the best investment you'll ever make as a leader. Reflect on how you spend your time as a leader:

- Do you take time to casually chat with team members before starting a meeting, or do you get right down to business without truly connecting? What is your reasoning?

  _____

  _____

  _____

  _____

  _____

- Next time you schedule 1:1 meetings, ask each direct report to create the agenda for their meeting with you. They can talk about anything they want—a goal, a vacation, a problem that may be impacting their work, whatever—it's their time. What is the result?

  _____

  _____

  _____

  _____

  _____

TRY IT THIS WEEK

Write about three ways you can help people in your department feel more connected to you. Then make it happen!

—⋅≻≻ ≺≺⋅—

SIMPLE TRUTH #9

Effective servant leaders realize they have to use different strokes for different folks.

ny leadership style will work in some situations but not in others. Yet half of all leaders use only one leadership style regardless of the situation. Leaders who use SLII®, our company's situational approach to effective leadership, know you can't treat everyone the same. SLII® leaders flex their style by using different strokes (leadership styles) for different folks depending on their development level in their present job.

First determine the person's development level. Then match it with the right leadership style to give them the help they need:

- Enthusiastic Beginners don't know how to do the job but are excited to get started. They need a Directive leadership style.

- Disillusioned Learners are still learning but feel discouraged and insecure. They need a Coaching leadership style.

- Capable, but Cautious, Contributors are getting the hang of things but still need occasional help. They need a Supportive leadership style.

- Self-Reliant Achievers are at the top of their game. They need a Delegating leadership style.

TRY IT THIS WEEK

Try using all four leadership styles: Give a new employee clear direction. Offer a frustrated employee both direction and encouragement. If someone is doing well but still asking questions, support their ideas. Finally, for someone who has their job all figured out, get out of their way, and let them be magnificent!

(Note: Scan the QR code to learn more about SLII®.)

—·≫⟩⟨≪·—

SIMPLE TRUTH #10

Effective servant leaders don't just use different strokes for *different* folks, they also use different strokes for the *same* folks.

Most experienced people are at a similar development level in many of their tasks and goals. Their leader can often use the same leadership style on that person (see Simple Truth #9). But everyone occasionally gets a task or goal that requires their leader to use a different leadership style. That's where SLII® shines.

Simple Truth #10

A situational leader is able to offer a matching leadership style to help every person succeed, regardless of their development level on a task or goal.

- Here's an example of matching leadership styles: A finance expert is anxious when dealing with people. His leader uses a Delegating style on financial matters, but when helping the person hone his people skills, the leader offers both direction and support—a Coaching style.

- Mismatched leadership styles look like this: A seasoned sales rep's new manager gives her unnecessarily specific direction on her sales tactics—a Directing style. But when she asks for help with her blog post, her manager uses a Supporting style, saying, "You'll do great. Call me if you need me."

TRY IT THIS WEEK

- Share the basics of SLII® (see Simple Truth #9) with your people. Help them realize they need different amounts of direction and support depending on their development level on a given task or goal. Write about their reaction.
- After you share SLII®, ask people to share their aha moments. In order for SLII® to be effective, it can't be done *to* people, it must be done *with* people.

(Note: Scan the QR code to learn more about SLII®.)

— ·}} {{· —

Profit is the applause you get for creating a motivating environment for your people so they will take good care of your customers.

A lot of people think the reason for being in business is to make a profit. While making a profit is important, leaders in high performing organizations know that when you take care of your people, they will turn around and take care of your customers. When that happens, your customers become part of your sales force, which takes care of the bottom line.

Explore the relationship between work environments and profits:

- Have you ever worked for an organization where profit is king and everything else comes in second? How did you feel about working in that kind of environment?

  _____

  _____

  _____

  _____

  _____

- If you want your people to make your customers their primary focus, how would you empower them to help make your vision a reality?

  _____

  _____

  _____

  _____

  _____

Remember, satisfied customers aren't enough. You need raving fans!

TRY IT THIS WEEK

As far as your customers are concerned, your company's frontline people *are* the company. Create a motivating environment for them by telling them how important they are, and help them turn customers into raving fans.

—∙≻≺∙—

Create autonomy through boundaries.

W hile it may sound counterintuitive, setting boundaries is the fastest way to empower people to become autonomous. Clear boundaries provide the guidance that people need to stay on track, make decisions, take initiative, and act like owners so they can reach both personal and organizational goals.

Here's how to create autonomy through boundaries (from *Empowerment Takes More Than a Minute*):

- Establish clear goals, expectations, and standards of performance. Communicate in plain language what people need to accomplish. Don't leave them on their own and then punish them when they don't meet your unspoken expectations.

- Ensure people are aware of all applicable policies and laws. Rules are important to guide day-to-day operations and decision-making.

- Confirm that everyone knows your organization's compelling vision (see Simple Truth #2). When people understand how their work fits into the big picture, it motivates them to perform better.

TRY IT THIS WEEK

Autonomous team members have the freedom to act. They are also more accountable for results. Do you feel confident enough in your leadership to begin taking steps toward a culture of empowerment? Why or why not?

—⟨⟨ ⟩⟩—

You get from people what you expect.

Unclear organizational expectations are a big obstacle to high performance. When someone isn't performing at their expected level, the cause may not be a lack of skill or motivation. They just might prioritize their tasks differently than you would. As a result, they may get in trouble for not doing tasks they didn't know they were supposed to do.

Our Top Ten Exercise bears this out: We ask an individual and their leader to make separate lists about the person's priorities. We've found that leaders tend to hold people accountable for end results (sales figures, customer surveys), but individuals focus more on routine things (to-do lists, spreadsheets, emails).

If you seldom discuss priorities with your team, try our Top Ten Exercise: Ask someone to list their top ten priorities. Separately, make your own list of their top ten priorities. Now compare. Usually only 20 percent of these lists will be aligned.

- Write about how you can ensure you are in sync with your people when it comes to expectations and priorities.

_____

_____

_____

_____

_____

_____

TRY IT THIS WEEK

Make discussions about priorities a priority! Have 1:1 meetings where each team member shares their top ten priorities with you, then work together on necessary adjustments. Leaders who are proactive in this area ensure expectations are clear on both sides.

—·⟩⟩⟨⟨·—

SIMPLE TRUTH #14

The best use of power is in service to others.

There's nothing wrong with being in a position of power if you use it properly. To quote seventeenth-century Spanish philosopher Baltasar Gracián, "The sole advantage of power is that you can do more good."

Lots of people struggle with the notion of authority. The abuse of power and the egoism associated with social and political sway have turned people off the entire concept. Instead of focusing on the power that comes with the title of leader, give your attention to the people you have an opportunity to serve.

Reflect on your own relationship with power:

- When you first became a leader, did you have a sense of being in a position of power? How did it make you feel?

- In a blog post entitled "If You Need to Be in Power You Probably Shouldn't Be," Randy wrote, "One of the paradoxes of leadership is that . . . placing others before ourselves and using our power to serve them actually brings us more power, respect, commitment, and loyalty." Write about how putting others first could bring you more power, respect, commitment, and loyalty.

TRY IT THIS WEEK

Do three things this week that exemplify this Simple Truth. Write about what you did and how it impacted your work environment.

(Note: You can read the rest of Randy's blog post at leadingwithtrust.com/2011/09/04/if-you-need-to-be-in-power/.)

—·✦❬❩✦·—

SIMPLE TRUTH #15

Never assume you know what motivates a person.

We've seen leaders get in trouble when they take for granted how people like to be motivated. You may not be surprised to know that lots of people are motivated by money—the more, the better. But many others aren't as interested in a big raise as they are in moving up the ladder into management or a higher level of leadership. And some folks aren't concerned about money or title—they are looking for a more people-oriented organizational culture where they feel psychologically safe, respected, and appreciated.

Answer these questions to gain insight on your internal motivations:

- When you were first starting out, what motivated you to work harder?

  _____

  _____

  _____

  _____

  _____

  _____

  _____

- How have your motivators changed over the years?

  _____

  _____

  _____

  _____

  _____

  _____

  _____

TRY IT THIS WEEK

In your next set of 1:1 meetings, ask team members about what motivates them to do good work. Then ask what the biggest motivating factor would be to make them stay with your organization. Write what you learn from their answers.

—·}} {{·—

People with humility don't think less of themselves, they just think of themselves less.

One thing that keeps people from becoming servant leaders is the human ego. Most people who appear to have a big ego have a hard time believing they are okay. They don't want to admit they are scared little kids inside.

What's the antidote for ego problems? It's humility. Most humble people have solid self-esteem—they are more focused on others than on themselves. Humility tames our judgmental nature and motivates us to reach out to support and encourage others. Author Fred Smith said, "People with humility don't deny their power; they just recognize that it passes through them, not from them."

Reflect on the role that humility has in your life:

- Write about a time when your ego prevented you from being a servant leader.

- Do you lead with humility? If so, write about how being humble helps you be a more effective leader.

TRY IT THIS WEEK

We all are occasionally self-focused. Make a concerted effort to exercise humility in place of ego this week. Practice putting the needs of others first. Ask people for ideas and feedback. Be intentionally kind and grateful to others. Write about your experience.

—⋆❥❥⋆—

It's okay to toot your own horn.

I t's no accident that this Simple Truth follows one about practicing humility. You can be a humble person and still be proud of yourself. It's perfectly okay to announce a personal or professional triumph to a family member, friend, or close colleague. And it's never wrong to catch yourself doing something right with a One Minute Praising, so put your right hand on your left shoulder and your left hand on your right shoulder, and give yourself a hug!

As a servant leader, you'll benefit from considering these questions about praise and pride:

- How do you react when you receive a compliment or expression of gratitude from someone?

  _____

  _____

  _____

  _____

  _____

- When someone you know talks about something they are proud of, do you see it as bragging, or are you happy for them? Do you feel the same way about sharing your own achievements?

  _____

  _____

  _____

  _____

  _____

  _____

TRY IT THIS WEEK

The way we choose to express pride can be a delicate balance in terms of how it may be perceived by others. Experiment at work and at home by telling someone about a small victory and watching how they react. If you aren't quite ready to do this, write about your comfort level with this concept.

─·﹥﹥﹤﹤·─

SIMPLE TRUTH #18

Don't work harder; work smarter.

Many managers say there aren't enough hours in the day to accomplish all that needs to be done. The problem is that these managers may be taking on work their people should be doing.

Instead of trying to do it all, help your people become self-reliant achievers. When you delegate effectively, you create time for your own tasks while empowering others. Use SLII® skills (see Simple Truths #9 and #10) to prepare, train, and develop your people. They'll bring their brains to work and use their innate knowledge, experience, and motivation to accomplish their goals.

Reflect on these questions to clarify the need for effective delegation:

- How might a leader who takes on tasks that a direct report could do cause problems in the future for both the leader and the direct report?

_____

_____

_____

- Fantasy time: if you had extra time during your workday to make progress on a project you really enjoy, what would that look like?

_____

_____

_____

TRY IT THIS WEEK

As you are working, make a note about which tasks you could delegate to others. Remember, some of your people may be hoping for a special assignment or may get excited about learning a new skill!

(Note: Scan the QR code to learn more about SLII®.)

—•❧❧•—

SIMPLE TRUTH #19

"No one of us is as smart as all of us."

—Eunice Parisi-Carew
and Don Carew

Too many leaders believe they're the smartest people in the office. They wouldn't think of collaborating with people who report to them. But today's workers are looking for trusting leaders who care about them and want their opinion. These people want to feel involved in contributing to the greater good.

Collaboration Begins with You, written by Ken, Jane Ripley, and Eunice Parisi-Carew, introduces the UNITE model with five elements for a collaborative culture: utilize differences; nurture safety and trust; involve others in crafting a clear purpose, values, and goals; talk openly; and empower yourself and others.

Reflect on times when your team members contributed to problem-solving:

- Leaders who involve their people come up with better solutions faster. Write about a time when one or more of your people helped solve a problem at work.

_____

_____

_____

_____

- How have you seen this Simple Truth come to life in your workplace?

_____

_____

_____

_____

TRY IT THIS WEEK

Write what this Simple Truth could do for you, your department, and your organization if you put it into action on a regular basis.

(Note: Scan the QR code or go to the Resources section to access the "Are You a Collaborative Leader?" assessment.)

—◆>⁺<◆—

SIMPLE TRUTH #20

Love is the answer.
What is the question?

We believe leadership is love. You may be familiar with this passage on love that is often recited at weddings:

Love is patient, love is kind. It does not envy, it does not
boast, it is not proud.
It does not dishonor others, it is not self-seeking, it is
not easily angered, it keeps no record of wrongs.
Love does not delight in evil but rejoices with the truth.
It always protects, always trusts, always hopes, always
perseveres.
Love never fails. (I Corinthians 13:4–7, 9)

In his book *The Greatest Thing in the World*, Scottish writer Henry Drummond (1851–1897) identified nine components of love based on this passage: patience, kindness, generosity, courtesy, humility, unselfishness, good temper, guilelessness, and sincerity. Reflect on what these words mean to you:

- If you could model these qualities in your leadership, what would the benefits be to you and your people?

  _____

  _____

  _____

  _____

  _____

- What does leading with love mean to you? Would you rather use a word other than *love* here?

  _____

  _____

  _____

  _____

  _____

TRY IT THIS WEEK

How do you see yourself living out these qualities in the daily choices you make with your team?

(Note: Scan the QR code or go to the Resources section to access the "Do You Lead with Love?" exercise.)

—◦❭❬◦—

Servant leaders don't command people to obey; they invite people to follow.

Most people don't like to be told to do something. They want to belong. They want to be included. Trusted servant leaders know people would rather follow a leader who invites team members to work beside them, not one who makes demands and looks down on them from above.

Consider the small, special ways you can connect with your team:

- Think of three specific ways you can model side-by-side leadership on a daily basis.

  _____

  _____

  _____

  _____

  _____

- Words matter! Strive to use the word *we* when talking with your people. For example, instead of saying "*I* want," say "*We* need." It instantly creates a feeling of working together as a cohesive team. Write about other small gestures you can make that could help people feel included.

  _____

  _____

  _____

  _____

  _____

TRY IT THIS WEEK

Focus on ways you can let your team members know how much you appreciate their contributions. Help them feel involved, and ask them what they think. Write about what you do and how people respond.

SIMPLE TRUTH #22

People who plan the battle rarely battle the plan.

Many leaders believe change will happen faster if they plan it and simply announce it to the workforce. This rarely happens. In fact, two-thirds of change initiatives fail. Yet the vast majority of companies still use a top-down approach that ignores the concerns of the people impacted by the change.

The best way to implement a change is to involve your people. Team members who have their concerns addressed are less likely to resist the change and more likely to see themselves as part of the organization's future.

Based on your experiences with organizational change, reflect on the following situations:

- Which would you rather commit to: a decision made by others that is being imposed on you or a decision made after you've had an opportunity to provide input? Why?

  _____

  _____

- Write about a time in your career when management made a sudden change that impacted your job. How did you react?

  _____

  _____

TRY IT THIS WEEK

Ask your leadership team these questions:

- Is our organization on track to achieve its vision?
- Are our people energized, committed, and passionate?
- Are our customers excited about our organization?

If they can't answer yes to all, consider a change strategy. (Note: scan the QR code to access the ebook *Five Communication Strategies That Make Leading Change Work*.)

—❧ ❧•—

SIMPLE TRUTH #23

Servant leaders love feedback.

lthough it doesn't come naturally for most people to give feedback to their manager, it's less tricky when the relationship is built on trust. If someone wants to tell you something, it means they care enough to give you honest and accurate data.

To prepare yourself for this week's Simple Truth, consider how you typically respond to feedback:

- Have you received positive or negative feedback from team members before? If you have, how did it feel?

  _____

  _____

- If you haven't, are you ready to tell your people you are interested in their feedback?

  _____

  _____

TRY IT THIS WEEK

Tell your team you see feedback as a gift and are open for 1:1 feedback sessions. Make it easy to connect and meet. Here are some tips to help people feel comfortable during these meetings:

- Thank the person and make it clear you're eager to hear their honest feedback. Remember, it takes courage for them to be there—and it may help you!
- It sounds odd, but try not to listen and think at the same time. Pay attention, ask questions, and take notes. Process the information later.
- Your reaction is important—you want to make the person feel welcome to schedule a feedback session anytime. Thank them again for coming to you.

—⋅≻≻⟨⟨⋅—

People who produce good results feel good about themselves.

P art of Ken's Leadership Point of View is "If I am living up to my expectations of myself as a leader, everything I do with you will be geared toward helping you produce good results and, in the process, feel good about yourself."

Acknowledging people's efforts and encouraging their progress sets up a positive cycle. Your praise helps people feel good about themselves, causing them to strive for good results, which triggers more good feelings. It's a win-win for both results and relationships!

Explore your feelings about the connection between results and positive self-esteem:

- Write about a time when you finished a big project or achieved a long-term goal. How did you feel about yourself immediately afterward? How do you feel looking back?

  _____

  _____

  _____

- Think about a manager whose primary goal is helping people feel good about themselves. Do you see yourself as that kind of leader? If not, what changes might you need to make?

  _____

  _____

  _____

TRY IT THIS WEEK

Read Ken's quote about what he expects of himself as a leader. Take action to help one of your team members produce good results that would make them feel good about themselves. Write about how it goes.

—❧❦·—

SIMPLE TRUTH #25

"It's not about you."

—Rick Warren

Rick Warren's quote "It's not about you" can be applied to so many circumstances, both at work and at home. Ken says, "To me, it means that it's okay for me to live my life as though I'm not a big deal. My job is to be kind, understanding, and loving to everyone I am around—to cheer them on and help them be the best person they can be."

Even servant leaders sometimes get caught up in ego issues. To keep yourself in check, reflect on these themes:

- Write how you would tell your team members they are the ones who make you look good, and you are here to serve them.

  _____

  _____

  _____

  _____

- Write about how you could focus more on others in every part of your life: at work, with family members, as a friend or colleague, or even in a brief chat with a stranger. It's not about you, it's about people you encounter every day.

  _____

  _____

  _____

  _____

Let's get our egos out of the way and focus on others, not ourselves. It could be the beginning of a beautiful world!

TRY IT THIS WEEK

Place sticky notes that say IT'S NOT ABOUT YOU in strategic places around your home and office where you will see them. Intentionally focus on others this week as often as this Simple Truth comes to mind. At the end of the week, write about this experiment and its effect on others—and yourself.

—•✥ ✥•—

SIMPLE TRUTH #26

Great leaders SERVE.

I n the book *The Secret: What Great Leaders Know and Do*, Mark Miller and Ken use the acronym SERVE to describe five key servant leader behaviors: see the future, engage and develop others, reinvent continuously, value results and relationships, and embody the values.

How would you answer the following questions regarding the various ways you SERVE as a leader?

- *See the future*—What do you want to be true in the future that is not true today?

  _____

- *Engage and develop others*—How can you help your people grow, as individuals and as a team?

  _____

- *Reinvent continuously*—What will your developmental focus be for the coming year?

  _____

- *Value results and relationships*—Do you tend to focus more on results or relationships? How can you achieve a better balance of the two areas?

  _____

- *Embody the values*—Which organizational values do you consistently model, and which do you need to work on?

  _____

TRY IT THIS WEEK

Write your answer to this question: Am I a serving leader or a self-serving leader? Give examples.

(Note: Read the book *The Secret: What Great Leaders Know and Do* to learn more about the SERVE model.)

PART TWO

—◆≫≪◆—

BUILDING TRUST

—⋅≫≪⋅—

SIMPLE TRUTH #27

Leadership begins with trust.

T rusted servant leaders understand that their number one priority is to build trust with their team. When you have the trust of your team, all things are possible. Without it, you're going to struggle to reach your goals.

Reflect on the following questions, and outline your game plan for building trust with your team this week:

- What would your team say are the top five ways you demonstrate your trustworthiness?

  _____
  _____
  _____
  _____

- How can you leverage your strengths to build more trust with your team this week?

  _____
  _____
  _____
  _____

- What would your team say are the top two ways you erode trust with your team? What can you do to address at least one of those areas of weakness?

  _____
  _____
  _____
  _____

TRY IT THIS WEEK

Complete this statement: A successful week of building trust with my team would look like _____.

Write about how you can make this happen and the end result.

—•≫≪•—

SIMPLE TRUTH #28

Building trust is a skill that can be learned and developed.

A person's perception of our trustworthiness is based on our behaviors. Trust is behaviorally based, which means it's a skill that can be learned and developed.

Leaders increase their trustworthiness based on behaviors that align with the four elements of trust, as illustrated in the ABCD model. Define what each behavior might look like.

- *Able*—Demonstrate competence.

  _____

  _____

- *Believable*—Act with integrity.

  _____

  _____

- *Connected*—Care about others.

  _____

  _____

- *Dependable*—Honor commitments.

  _____

  _____

TRY IT THIS WEEK

Practice these behaviors with your people this week. Write about your perceptions of how each behavior, when developed, can potentially build trust within your team.

(Note: Scan the QR code or go to the Resources section to access the "Are You a Trustworthy Leader?" assessment.)

—◦⟫⟨◦—

"Self-trust is the first secret of success."

—Ralph Waldo Emerson

S elf-trust starts with having a confident belief in your leadership mission. The best way to get clear on your mission as a leader is to develop your Leadership Point of View (LPOV). A clear understanding of your LPOV turbocharges your effectiveness as a leader and gives you the confident self-belief that you are making a difference with those you influence.

Think of your LPOV as a story about you and how you show up as a leader. People remember and respond more to stories than to a list of general principles about effective leadership. When others know your story, they can more easily understand your intentions, and they will come to know you on a deeper, more personal level.

The first step toward the creation of your LPOV is to thoughtfully consider your answers to these questions:

- What people and events have had a major influence on who you are today as a person and a leader?

_____

- What key values have shaped your behavior over time?

_____

- What do you expect of others, and what can others expect of you as a leader?

_____

TRY IT THIS WEEK

Start working on an outline for your own LPOV by following the steps in the "Creating Your Leadership Point of View" exercise. Remember, it doesn't pay to rush through this activity. Don't expect to finish it this week. Enjoy the process.

(Note: Scan the QR code or go to the Resources section to access the "Creating Your Leadership Point of View" exercise.)

—•≫≪•—

Someone must make the first move to extend trust. Leaders go first.

Trust can't grow until someone extends it. Most leaders tend to think they are automatically trusted by others because of their position or title. The truth is that leaders have the responsibility to first extend trust to their people, which in turn allows them to demonstrate their own trustworthiness.

Reflect on these prompts to develop your game plan for this week:

1. Identify a situation where you need to extend trust to someone.
2. What about the person or situation gives you confidence to extend trust? (Think of how the person demonstrates the ABCD behaviors shown in Simple Truth #28.)
3. What gives you cause for concern?
4. Think about how you can extend trust to them while also addressing your areas of concern.

TRY IT THIS WEEK

Outline a conversation with the person you chose above.

1. Open by expressing confidence in their trustworthiness.
2. Discuss your areas of concern; listen generously to their viewpoint.
3. Describe how to resolve the areas of concern.
4. Gain their agreement, and confirm the next steps.

Conduct this conversation and reflect on the experience. What worked well? What might you do differently next time?

—•≫≺•—

SIMPLE TRUTH #31

"People admire your strengths, but they respect your honesty regarding your vulnerability."

—Colleen Barrett

isplaying vulnerability is critical to becoming a trusted servant leader. People want to know the person behind the title or position—and the only way for that to happen is for you to share information about yourself. Opening up to your team can be uncomfortable, but the results of higher trust are worth it!

Two primary ways to be more vulnerable are to share information about yourself and ask for feedback. Here are some examples of topics to share and inquire about:

- Share a childhood memory and why it's important to you.
- Share about an important mentor in your life.
- Share what keeps you up at night.
- Share what you learned about trust (positive or negative) from your parents.
- Ask people what you can do more effectively to build trust with them.
- Ask people how they feel about giving you feedback.
- Ask people what they think is most important to you in life.
- Ask people how they think you feel about being a leader.

TRY IT THIS WEEK

Review the above list of share-and-ask items and select ones to use this week to show a more personal side of yourself.

SIMPLE TRUTH #32

There's no trust without *us*.

In its purest and most basic form, trust is a psychological and emotional construct between two people. It's a willingness to be vulnerable with another person without fear of being taken advantage of or harmed. When two people are willing to trust each other, they are committing to the *us* in trust.

One of the best ways to develop trust with someone at work is to have a conversation to help you get to know each other on a more personal level. Consider trading responses to some of these questions, or make up your own. The lines are to get you started.

- What excites you about life right now?

  _____

- Who is your hero?

  _____

- What is one of your favorite childhood memories?

  _____

- What is your favorite movie? Book? Sport? Hobby?

  _____

- If you could choose any career, what would it be?

  _____

- What is your dream vacation?

  _____

TRY IT THIS WEEK

Identify a colleague you'd like to know better. Schedule a "getting to know you Q&A" meeting, break, or lunch with them. Let them know there are no strings attached and they are welcome to ask you questions. Write about how it goes.

—·≫≫ ≪≪·—

Fear is the enemy of trust.

We experience fear whenever our well-being is threatened. Safety, on the other hand, is the opposite of fear. We feel safe when we trust our environment and the people in it, giving us confidence and security.

If you think fear may be affecting people in your workplace, consider these approaches:

- Have a conversation with the person or team in question about the root cause or issue, and brainstorm what can be done to reduce or eliminate fear.
- Be consistent. Inconsistent behavior breeds doubt and fear and erodes trust.
- Treat mistakes as learning moments. Rather than assigning blame, examine what was learned and what can be done differently in the future.
- Explain the reason behind decisions to remove suspicion and doubt, which are the seeds of fear.
- Communicate clearly and openly. Clear communication reduces misunderstanding, and sharing information shows that you trust people with knowing the details.
- Focus on the present. Fear often stems from negative past experiences or worries about the future.

TRY IT THIS WEEK

Identify a relationship where fear is eroding trust, and address it using some of these strategies.

A relationship with no trust is like a cell phone with no service or internet—all you can do is play games.

If you're a leader of a remote team, some of your people may have a mental image not of you but of the person they perceive you to be. This image is formed through encounters as random as emails, videos, speeches, online meetings, or stories from others. Until they get to know the *real* you, they won't know whether you are sincere or just playing games.

You can help people get to know the authentic you by being REAL: reveal, engage, acknowledge, listen. Use this acronym to outline how you can display more authenticity this week:

- Reveal information about yourself.

  _____

  _____

- Engage employees as individuals.

  _____

  _____

- Acknowledge employee contributions.

  _____

  _____

- Listen to learn.

  _____

  _____

TRY IT THIS WEEK

Whom will you reach out to and how will you show them your authentic self? Complete the "Be REAL" worksheet, and decide on your game plan for this week.

(Note: Scan the QR code or go to the Resources section to access the "Be REAL" worksheet.)

—·⧫⧫·—

People don't care how much you know until they know how much you care.

L eaders commonly assume that being the highest-ranking person in the room earns the trust and respect of others. That's a mistake. People grant you their trust when they believe you care about them and intend to act in ways that respect and value their personal welfare.

Most leaders we've met have good intentions and value their team members, but they often fall short of explicitly and proactively demonstrating care and concern for them.

Reflect on the following strategies for expressing care. Select a few, describe what you would do, and create a plan to act on your good intentions.

- Perform a random act of kindness for someone.

  _____

- Praise a colleague to their leader.

  _____

- Reach out to someone in their time of need.

  _____

- Write a note of appreciation to someone.

  _____

- Pay attention to nonverbals: do your tone of voice and body language match your intent?

  _____

- Listen with the intent of being influenced.

  _____

- Socialize with a colleague or team member outside of work.

  _____

- Create opportunities to interact with others more often.

  _____

TRY IT THIS WEEK

Finish this sentence: I will demonstrate care and concern by

_____.

—·》〈·—

"People will forget what you said, people will forget what you did, but people will never forget how you made them feel."

—Maya Angelou

O ne of the greatest measures of your influence as a leader is the answer to this question: Are my people better off because of my presence in their life?

If the answer is an unequivocal yes, bravo! If not, consider what you can do differently. As we advocate in *Simple Truths of Leadership*, play show-and-tell with your team.

To show you care, do the following:

- Value people's competence. Solicit their input when making decisions and invest in their skill development by supporting ongoing training.
- Demonstrate integrity. Act in alignment with personal and organizational values. Treat people fairly and respectfully.
- Express care and concern. This is one of the easiest ways for leaders to earn the trust and respect of their team.

To tell people you care, do the following:

- Praise and reward good performance.
- Offer coaching and feedback to help people improve their performance.
- Be truthful. Don't spin the truth or omit key details.
- Share information about yourself. Being vulnerable and transparent builds trust with others.

TRY IT THIS WEEK

Play show-and-tell at work, and write about it.

—·❥❦·—

"Your actions speak so loudly I cannot hear what you are saying."

—Anonymous

Integrity is at the heart of being a trusted servant leader. In fact, we would argue it's impossible for someone to be a servant leader if they lack integrity. Walking your talk—when your actions align with your speech—is a key aspect of being a leader with integrity.

As a trusted servant leader, you should display your integrity every day. Give examples of how you would demonstrate the following signs of integrity:

- You treat people ethically and fairly.

  _____

- Your behavior reflects your personal values.

  _____

- You admit your mistakes.

  _____

- You don't say one thing and do another.

  _____

- You honor your commitments.

  _____

Several other important characteristics of integrity are worth mentioning, and we've included some of them in the "Do You Lead with Integrity?" assessment.

TRY IT THIS WEEK

Finish this sentence: I will act with integrity this week by _____. Write about the end result.

(Note: Scan the QR code or go to the Resources section to access the "Do You Lead with Integrity?" assessment.)

—◦⟩⟩⟨⟨◦—

Tell the truth. Always. It's that simple.

The great American author and humorist Mark Twain opined that many people must regard truth as their most valuable possession since they are so economical in its use.

Telling the truth—perhaps there is nothing as difficult as this most simple of leadership truths. Yielding to the temptation to be less than honest leads to what Randy calls "truth decay."

Here are a few common scenarios:

- *Withholding information*—This makes people feel they aren't trusted to use information responsibly.
- *Not walking your talk*—When this happens, followers quickly learn that the leader can't be trusted.
- *Dropping balls*—Not following through on commitments is a leading contributor to truth decay.
- *Gossiping*—Any followers who observe this behavior will wonder, "If they gossip about others, are they talking about me too?"

As you consider your game plan this week, think about situations where you experience truth decay—and what you can do to prevent it.

TRY IT THIS WEEK

Identify and write about a situation where you may be tempted to not be 100 percent truthful. What will you do to tell the truth in a candid yet caring manner?

—·❯❯❮❮·—

SIMPLE TRUTH #39

Don't ever make a promise you can't keep.

A promise given is an expectation created. One of the primary ways we erode trust with others is when we fail to meet their expectations. Think back to when you were a child and an adult you trusted made a promise they didn't keep. Do you remember how disappointed you felt?

Few people wake up in the morning and say to themselves, "I can't wait to break my promises today!" Most have the intention to deliver on their commitments, but they don't always have a plan. There is truth in the old adage "People don't plan to fail; they just fail to plan."

Trusted servant leaders follow through on their promises. Examine examples from your own leadership:

- Write about a time in your career when you didn't keep a promise.

  _____

- How can you ensure this won't happen in the future?

  _____

TRY IT THIS WEEK

Create a plan to follow through on a promise you've made based on answers to the following questions:

- What is the commitment?
- What is the deadline?
- What tasks do you need to complete prior to the deadline?
- What resources do you need?
- What steps do you need to take to accomplish the goal?
- What obstacles may keep you from accomplishing the goal?
- What can you do to eliminate these obstacles?

—•≫≻≺≪•—

SIMPLE TRUTH #40

"There's nothing so unequal as the equal treatment of unequals."

—Anonymous

Many leaders think they are being fair when they treat everyone the same. But treating everyone the same regardless of their needs or situation can be one of the most unfair things a leader can do.

Each person should be treated equitably and ethically.
Treat people equitably by doing any of the following:

- Be respectful and acknowledge their basic dignity.
- Show empathy for their life situation.
- Solicit and value their contributions.
- Give recognition and rewards for their accomplishments.
- Consider their input when making decisions.

Treat people ethically by doing any of the following:

- Be honest, trustworthy, and accountable.
- Put other peoples' interests ahead of your own.
- Do the right thing, even when it is hard or inconvenient.
- Don't gossip or talk about others behind their backs.
- Stand up for the rights of others.

TRY IT THIS WEEK

Choose one or more of the items above and commit to doing it this week when dealing with others. Write about what happens.

—•⟩⟩⟨⟨•—

SIMPLE TRUTH #41

#Trust is always trending. Doing the right thing never goes out of style.

People in our social-media-fueled culture are fascinated by viral trends. Funny cat videos, crazy dance routines, or household hacks regularly make the rounds—and a number of people have somehow carved out a lucrative living generating content that goes viral.

Although upstanding leadership behavior rarely makes an appearance on social media channels, servant leaders know that #Trust is always trending. Knowing your values and living in alignment with them is essential for being a trusted servant leader.

Here's a fun way to discover your true north through your personal values as a trusted servant leader.

1. Write a list of qualities that have meaning for you.
2. Narrow down the values on that list to the ten most important.
3. When you're finished, choose your top three to five.
4. Rank those top values in order.

To further explore your personal vision and values, see the "Your Personal Compelling Vision" exercise.

TRY IT THIS WEEK

Write a behavioral example of how you live out each of your top values. Complete this sentence: I am living according to this value whenever I _____.

(Note: Scan the QR code or go to the Resources section to access the "Your Personal Compelling Vision" exercise.)

—◦≻⟩⟨≺◦—

SIMPLE TRUTH #42

True servant leaders admit their mistakes.

Too many leaders think admitting mistakes is a sign of weakness. On the contrary—owning up to your shortcomings is one of the most powerful and effective ways to build, or rebuild, trust with others.

Most people want leaders who are sincere. They know their leader isn't perfect and doesn't have all the answers, despite some leaders' attempts to act otherwise. As a leader, don't let your ego hijack common sense the next time you make a mistake. Own it, learn from it, and do better next time.

Reflect on a time when you were less than straightforward about admitting you made an error:

- What happened? Was someone else blamed for your mistake?

  _____

  _____

- Did the truth eventually come out? How did you feel?

  _____

  _____

TRY IT THIS WEEK

Take the following steps this week:

1. Identify a recent mistake you didn't admit to.
2. Own it. Write how you could communicate your responsibility for the mistake and any harm or inconvenience it may have caused others.
3. Highlight the lesson. Write what you learned and how it will impact your behavior in the future.
4. If you choose, share steps 2 and 3 in a conversation with your peers or team members.

—•⟫⟪•—

Since we were given two ears and one mouth, we should listen more than we speak.

L istening is one of the most powerful—yet underrated—leadership skills. When people are asked to describe their best boss, what quality always appears on the list? Being a good listener.

A simple way to improve your listening skills is to follow the EAR model:

- *Explore*—Occasionally ask questions to clarify your understanding and probe deeper until you truly understand what the other person is trying to communicate.
- *Acknowledge*—At appropriate times in the conversation, acknowledge the other person's viewpoint and rephrase what they're saying. This shows the other person you're paying attention.
- *Respond*—After you're through exploring and acknowledging, respond with your own thoughts and ideas.

TRY IT THIS WEEK

Identify an important conversation you need to have with someone. Use the EAR model to plan your conversation.

- Explore with helpful phrases: "Tell me more." "Can you clarify what you mean by that?"
- Acknowledge with helpful phrases: "What you're saying is . . ." "If I understand correctly . . ."
- Respond with helpful phrases: "I think . . ." "It seems like . . ."

—❖❖❖—

The most important part of leadership is what happens when you're not there.

High-control leaders have difficulty delegating work to others. This prevents direct reports from developing to higher levels of performance and can result in leaders burning out. Delegating tasks fosters confidence in individuals and builds trusting relationships.

If you are the kind of leader who feels like you can never take a vacation because you always have to be available for your team, answer these questions:

- Are the people on your team competent at their jobs?

- Are they straightforward with you and each other?

- Do they seem to care about each other?

- Are they dependable and committed to doing a great job?

Sometimes when a leader expresses confidence and extends trust to people, it becomes a self-fulfilling prophecy.

TRY IT THIS WEEK

Follow this plan to become more proficient at delegating work to others.

1. Make sure the goal is clear and the person knows what a good job looks like so they can hit the target.
2. Assess the competence and commitment of the person on the task. Make sure they have the knowledge, skills, and motivation to accomplish the goal.
3. Clarify the boundaries of responsibility so the individual knows their level of authority regarding things like budget, decision-making, and approval process.
4. Be available! Delegation does not mean abdication. Stay in regular contact and assist as needed.

─•⟩⟩⟨⟨•─

SIMPLE TRUTH #45

The opposite of trust is not distrust— it's control.

W hy is trust the opposite of control? It's because trust involves taking a risk and making yourself vulnerable to others' actions. Control is a way to reduce that risk.

The following are strategies you can use to replace the need for control with trusting others:

- *Delegate*—Allow others to take responsibility and ownership of the task, which can help you focus on other things (see Simple Truth #44).
- *Let go of perfectionism*—Trying to make everything perfect can be exhausting and unrealistic. Letting go of the need for perfection can help you feel more relaxed.
- *Accept*—There will always be aspects of life you can't control. Accepting that fact can help you move forward with peace of mind and focus on what you need to do.
- *Communicate*—Sharing your needs and expectations helps people understand their roles and enables them to work with you on your goals.
- *Pray, meditate, or practice mindfulness*—Engaging in these practices can help you be less concerned about who is in control and more aware of your thoughts and emotions.

TRY IT THIS WEEK

Pick one of the above strategies to help you learn to relinquish control. Write about it.

—•≫≪•—

People don't resist change; they resist being controlled.

Change in the workplace always elicits concerns. Leaders often assume that people will automatically resist the change, so they go into overdrive to convince people to accept it. It's not that people are resistant to change; it's that they don't like being controlled.

No one wants to be told to change and be forced to go along with it—they'd rather be part of the change process. When people are involved in the change process, they take more ownership over the outcome.

Once your team learns of an impending change, schedule either 1:1 or team meetings to address people's concerns. At these meetings, your task is to listen, surface concerns, and solicit ideas—not to convince or control. Ask the following questions to gain more insight:

- In general, what are your concerns about this change?
- What additional information would be most helpful?
- What do you think the organization is trying to accomplish with this change?
- How do people you respect feel about this change?
- How do you think this change will impact you personally?
- How do you want to be involved in this change?

TRY IT THIS WEEK

Have a concerns conversation with someone you need to influence regarding a change. Write about what happened at this meeting.

—⋅⟩⟩⟨⟨⋅—

People without accurate information cannot act responsibly, but people with accurate information are compelled to act responsibly.

I n some organizations, information is viewed and treated as power. Those who have it often use it to control people and circumstances, which leaves those without information and power handicapped in their ability to be proactive and accomplish work on their own.

Trusted servant leaders openly share information so that others are empowered to make decisions in the best interests of the organization. Few things say "I trust you" more than giving people access to critical information. It shows that you believe they are responsible enough to use the information in the right way for the right purposes.

To prepare yourself and your team for an information-sharing meeting, first identify specific information, such as reports, financial data, or performance metrics, and then consider the following questions:

- Which of these information sources could be shared with your people (perhaps with appropriate editing) to empower them to make more decisions on their own?

  _____

  _____

  _____

  _____

- What parameters do you need to set up to ensure people clearly understand how and when to use this information?

  _____

  _____

  _____

  _____

TRY IT THIS WEEK

Create a plan to share this information and to train your team on its use.

—◦≫≪◦—

SIMPLE TRUTH #48

Building trust is a journey, not a destination.

Think of a time in your life when you took a long journey. Maybe it was a family road trip or a multistop flight. Chances are you encountered some unexpected delays or detours along the way.

The same is true in our journey of building trust. There are twists and turns as we grow in trust with others. Sometimes we cruise along when trust is flourishing, and other times we have a fender bender and trust takes a hit.

Don't let relational fender benders stop you from continuing to build trust with others. When trust takes a hit, you need a plan to get it back on track.

Following the "Acknowledge, Apologize, Act" process outlined below will help you restore eroded trust.

Identify a person and situation where you may have eroded trust. Outline a conversation with this person. Consider the following steps, then follow through with a 1:1 meeting:

1. Open the conversation.
2. Acknowledge: confirm how you broke trust (see the ABCD model described in Simple Truth #28).
3. Apologize: express remorse and ask for a fresh start.
4. Act: ask yourself what commitments you can make to change your behavior to restore trust.

TRY IT THIS WEEK

Write about the experience above. How did you feel before, during, and after the meeting?

—·✕ ✕·—

A successful apology is essential in rebuilding trust.

The apology can be a make-it-or-break-it moment in rebuilding trust. If done well, it sets the stage for trust to be restored. If done poorly, trust can be damaged even further. That's why it's critical to know how to deliver an effective apology.

Identify a person you need to apologize to. Review the following characteristics of effective apologies and consider how you can use them to apologize:

1. Pick the right time when the person will be receptive to hearing your apology.
2. Admit your role in the situation.
3. Accept responsibility for your actions.
4. Express remorse for any pain, harm, or inconvenience you caused the other person.
5. Be sincere and express empathy for how you impacted the other person.
6. Don't use conditional words like *if* or *but*.
7. Don't make excuses or blame other people or circumstances.
8. Resist the urge to offer explanations unless asked. Explaining can sound like excuse making.
9. Listen to the other person's thoughts and feelings.
10. Commit to not repeating the behavior.

TRY IT THIS WEEK

If you have been waiting to apologize to someone, schedule a meeting and have this conversation as soon as you can. If no apologies are necessary right now, practice these steps in front of a mirror.

—⋅❯❯⋊⋉❮⋅—

SIMPLE TRUTH #50

Apologizing is not necessarily an admission of guilt, but it is an admission of responsibility.

We've seen a fair number of people bristle at accepting that an apology is an admission only of responsibility, not guilt. Their initial reaction tends to be "I'm not going to apologize because I didn't do anything wrong!" We can understand that position because none of us likes to take the blame for something we didn't do. However, being a trusted servant leader means having the wisdom to know when to put your ego aside and do what's best for the health of the relationship.

This Simple Truth is all about accepting responsibility for healing a fractured relationship instead of fighting over who's right and who's wrong.

Reflect on the following questions:

- How do you feel about the concept that servant leaders should take the blame if their team fails on a project or initiative?

  _____

  _____

  _____

  _____

- Is being accountable for their people's mistakes the responsibility of a servant leader?

  _____

  _____

  _____

  _____

- Are you withholding an apology because you're insisting the other person take the blame?

  _____

  _____

  _____

  _____

TRY IT THIS WEEK

Write about the idea of apologizing when you believe the other person is in the wrong.

—·⟫⟪·—

Choosing not to forgive someone is like taking poison and waiting for the other person to die.

People will break your trust. It's not a question of *if* but *when*. Those occasions are choice points. We can choose to let the pain take root and poison us from the inside out, or we can choose to forgive and move forward in freedom and healing.

Leaders need to have thick skin and a soft heart. That's a principle Randy learned early in his leadership journey. When people break our trust, we need to have skin thick enough to absorb the blow but a heart soft enough to have compassion and forgiveness toward those people.

Identify a person whom you've been refusing to forgive. Reflect upon the following points and consider how you'd like to respond:

- Are you waiting for the other person to earn your forgiveness? If so, consider that forgiveness is something that must be offered by you; it can't be earned by the other person.

_____

_____

_____

_____

- Are you waiting to forgive the other person until they make amends? Remember, forgiveness is your choice regardless of whether the other person makes amends.

_____

_____

_____

_____

TRY IT THIS WEEK

Write about your feelings on these concepts. Include experiences you or someone you know may have had in this area.

—◦꙳꙳◦—

SIMPLE TRUTH #52

Forgiveness is letting go of all hope for a better past.

S uffering a betrayal of trust can be one of the most challenging times in your life. And choosing to forgive may seem impossible. Myths about forgiveness persist, such as that it signifies weakness and lets the offending party off the hook. Don't believe them. Forgiveness involves letting go of the past so you can move forward in freedom.

By reminding ourselves what forgiveness is and isn't, we can open ourselves to greater connections with our teams:

- Forgiveness is a choice, not a feeling or attitude. You don't have to wait until you feel like forgiving someone.
- Forgiving doesn't mean forgetting.
- Forgiveness doesn't eliminate consequences.
- Forgiving doesn't make you a weakling or a doormat. Forgiveness shows maturity and depth of character.
- Forgiveness isn't a way to avoid pain. Take time to process your feelings and make a clear decision.
- Forgiveness is not a weapon. Once you forgive someone, don't use their past behavior as a tool to harm them.
- Forgiveness is freedom. Withholding it drains your energy and negatively colors your outlook on life.

TRY IT THIS WEEK

Identify a person you need to forgive. Reflecting on the principles listed above may help.

Closing Thoughts

Congratulations on completing your journey through *Simple Truths of Leadership Playbook*!

Whenever you reach a notable milestone, it's good to reflect on what you've learned and celebrate your accomplishments.

When you think back to where you started and where you are now as a trusted servant leader, what has been most challenging? What has been most rewarding? What advice would you give to someone striving to be a servant leader and build trust with others?

Finally, how are you going to celebrate your progress? As you know, trusted servant leaders look for every opportunity to catch their people doing something right, so apply that truth to yourself and find a way to commemorate all your hard work.

Keep serving and building trust,

Ken and Randy

Resources

Simple Truths of Leadership Self-Assessment

When working toward completion of a task or goal, we all move along a continuum of four development levels:

- *Enthusiastic Beginner* (D1)—You have low competence and high commitment. You don't know how to do this task but are excited to get started. You need a Directive leadership style.
- *Disillusioned Learner* (D2)—You have some competence and low commitment. You are still learning but are feeling discouraged and insecure. You need a Coaching leadership style.
- *Capable, but Cautious, Contributor* (D3)—You have high competence and variable commitment. You are getting the hang of things but still need occasional help. You need a Supportive leadership style.
- *Self-Reliant Achiever* (D4)—You have high competence and high commitment. You are at the top of your game on this task. You need a Delegating leadership style.

Using the basics of SLII®, determine your development level on each of the 52 Simple Truths and check the box that applies to your stage of development. We suggest you do this at least twice: once when you are beginning to study the Simple Truth and again when you feel you have achieved success in that area. Feel free to check your progress as you go along.

For more details on SLII® and how to determine your development level, see Simple Truths #9, #10, and #18.

Simple Truth #	Concept	D1	D2	D3	D4
	PART ONE: SERVANT LEADERSHIP				
1	Servant leadership is the best way to achieve both great results and great relationships.				
2	Every great organization has a compelling vision.				
3	Servant leaders turn the traditional pyramid upside down.				
4	All good performance starts with clear goals.				
5	The key to developing people is to catch them doing something right.				
6	Praise progress!				
7	When people are off track, don't reprimand them—redirect them.				

Simple Truth #	Concept	D1	D2	D3	D4
8	The best minute servant leaders spend is the one they invest in people.				
9	Effective servant leaders realize they have to use different strokes for different folks.				
10	Effective servant leaders don't just use different strokes for *different* folks, they also use different strokes for the *same* folks.				
11	Profit is the applause you get for creating a motivating environment for your people so they will take good care of your customers.				
12	Create autonomy through boundaries.				
13	You get from people what you expect.				
14	The best use of power is in service to others.				
15	Never assume you know what motivates a person.				
16	People with humility don't think less of themselves, they just think of themselves less.				

Simple Truth #	Concept	D1	D2	D3	D4
17	It's okay to toot your own horn.				
18	Don't work harder; work smarter.				
19	"No one of us is as smart as all of us."—Eunice Parisi-Carew and Don Carew				
20	Love is the answer. What is the question?				
21	Servant leaders don't command people to obey; they invite people to follow.				
22	People who plan the battle rarely battle the plan.				
23	Servant leaders love feedback.				
24	People who produce good results feel good about themselves.				
25	"It's not about you."—Rick Warren				
26	Great leaders SERVE.				
	PART TWO: BUILDING TRUST				
27	Leadership begins with trust.				

Simple Truth #	Concept	D1	D2	D3	D4
28	Building trust is a skill that can be learned and developed.				
29	"Self-trust is the first secret of success."—Ralph Waldo Emerson				
30	Someone must make the first move to extend trust. Leaders go first.				
31	"People admire your strengths, but they respect your honesty regarding your vulnerability."—Colleen Barrett				
32	There's no trust without *us*.				
33	Fear is the enemy of trust.				
34	A relationship with no trust is like a cell phone with no service or internet—all you can do is play games.				
35	People don't care how much you know until they know how much you care.				
36	"People will forget what you said, people will forget what you did, but people will never forget how you made them feel."—Maya Angelou				

Simple Truth #	Concept	D1	D2	D3	D4
37	"Your actions speak so loudly I cannot hear what you are saying." —Anonymous				
38	Tell the truth. Always. It's that simple.				
39	Don't ever make a promise you can't keep.				
40	"There's nothing so unequal as the equal treatment of unequals." —Anonymous				
41	#Trust is always trending. Doing the right thing never goes out of style.				
42	True servant leaders admit their mistakes.				
43	Since we were given two ears and one mouth, we should listen more than we speak.				
44	The most important part of leadership is what happens when you're not there.				
45	The opposite of trust is not distrust—it's control.				
46	People don't resist change; they resist being controlled.				

Simple Truth #	Concept	D1	D2	D3	D4
47	People without accurate information cannot act responsibly, but people with accurate information are compelled to act responsibly.				
48	Building trust is a journey, not a destination.				
49	A successful apology is essential in rebuilding trust.				
50	Apologizing is not necessarily an admission of guilt, but it is an admission of responsibility.				
51	Choosing not to forgive someone is like taking poison and waiting for the other person to die.				
52	Forgiveness is letting go of all hope for a better past.				

Servant leadership is the best way to achieve both great results and great relationships.

Are You a Servant Leader but Don't Know It?

Take our quiz to find out how well you demonstrate the qualities of servant leadership. If you can check off more than six statements, you are well on your way to being a trusted servant leader!

- ☐ People would say I take time to understand their perspective before sharing my own.
- ☐ People would say I am fully present when working with them: I remove distractions, look up, and listen to what they are saying.
- ☐ People would say I create an environment that welcomes, celebrates, and values people's authenticity and differences.
- ☐ People would say I listen to learn when others are speaking to me.
- ☐ People would say I invest in the development of others.
- ☐ People would say I create a trusting work environment.
- ☐ People would say I seek others' opinions and regularly ask for input and feedback.
- ☐ People would say I enjoy catching people doing things right.

- [ ] People would say I provide honest, constructive feedback to them.
- [ ] People would say I am conscious of the impact my actions have on others.
- [ ] People would say I tell the truth.
- [ ] People would say I act with their best interests in mind.

Total checked _____

SIMPLE TRUTH #2:
Every great organization has a compelling vision.

Your Personal Compelling Vision

Before you can have a compelling vision for your organization, it helps if you create a compelling vision for yourself. Here's how!

Creating Your Personal Purpose Statement

Let's start by creating your personal purpose statement, which describes who you are. (Susan Fowler developed this process for Blanchard's Self Leadership program.)

1. List some personal characteristics you feel good about. These will be nouns. Here are some examples:

charm	computer expertise	creativity
energy	enthusiasm	good looks
happiness	mechanical aptitude	patience
people skills	physical strength	sales ability

_____

_____

_____

_____

2. List ways you successfully interact with people. These will be verbs. Here are some examples:

act   educate   encourage
help   lead   love
manage   motivate   plan
produce   study   teach

_____

_____

_____

_____

3. Visualize what your perfect world looks like. What are the people doing and saying? Write a description of this perfect world. For example, "My perfect world is a place where people know their destinations and are enjoying their life journeys."

_____

_____

_____

4. Combine two of your nouns, two of your verbs, and your definition of your perfect world to come up with your purpose statement. For example, "My life purpose is to use my energy and my people skills to teach and motivate people to know their destinations and enjoy their life journeys."

_____

_____

_____

Determining Your Personal Picture of the Future

Now, let's work on visualizing where you are going. (Margie Blanchard developed this fantasy Friday experience for Blanchard.) Write a paragraph about your "fantasy Friday" ten years from now. This fantasy Friday is still a workday, but it's also the beginning of the weekend. Answer these questions:

1. Where are you living?
2. With whom?
3. What are you doing throughout the day, hour by hour?
4. What are you feeling throughout the day—socially, emotionally, physically, spiritually?

_____

_____

_____

_____

_____

_____

_____

Values Exercise Part A: Determining Your Personal Values

To start the process of determining your personal values (what will guide your journey), circle ten values from the list below that mean the most to you personally. Feel free to add your own values that are not on this list.

Accountability	Fulfillment	Peace
Achievement	Fun	Persistence
Adaptability	Generosity	Play
Authenticity	Growth	Power
Belonging	Happiness	Productivity
Caring	Hard work	Profitability
Clarity	Harmony	Prosperity
Collaboration	Honesty	Quality
Commitment	Hope	Recognition
Community	Hospitality	Relationships
Compassion	Humor	Resourcefulness
Competitiveness	Independence	Respect
Control	Influence	Responsibility
Creativity	Initiative	Security
Curiosity	Innovation	Service
Dependability	Integrity	Simplicity
Discipline	Intelligence	Sincerity
Duty	Involvement	Success
Efficiency	Joy	Synergy
Empathy	Justice	Teamwork
Equality	Learning	Trust
Excellence	Love	Wisdom
Excitement	Loyalty	_____
Expressiveness	Openness	_____
Fairness	Originality	_____
Flexibility	Passion	
Friendship	Patience	

Values Exercise Part B: Determining Your Top Five Values

The next step is to narrow down your top values.

1. Write each of the ten values that you chose in part A next to a number in the box below.

1. _____	6. _____
2. _____	7. _____
3. _____	8. _____
4. _____	9. _____
5. _____	10. _____

2. One by one, compare the numbered value to all others, circling which one you value more from the pair. Total the number of circles chosen for each value, and write that total below.

```
1  2
1  3   2  3
1  4   2  4   3  4
1  5   2  5   3  5   4  5
1  6   2  6   3  6   4  6   5  6
1  7   2  7   3  7   4  7   5  7   6  7
1  8   2  8   3  8   4  8   5  8   6  8   7  8
1  9   2  9   3  9   4  9   5  9   6  9   7  9   8  9
1 10   2 10   3 10   4 10   5 10   6 10   7 10   8 10   9 10
```

Totals:

___	___	___	___	___	___	___	___	___	___
1	2	3	4	5	6	7	8	9	10

3. Now rank your top five values beginning with the value with the highest total.

1. _____
2. _____
3. _____
4. _____
5. _____

Values Exercise Part C: Defining Your Values

Finally, write a sentence that reflects how your behaviors are congruent with each of your values. For example: "I value joy and know I am living by this value anytime I let my playful inner child express himself."

I value _____ and know I am living by this value

_____

I value _____ and know I am living by this value

_____

I value _____ and know I am living by this value

_____

I value _____ and know I am living by this value

_____

I value _____ and know I am living by this value

_____

"No one of us is as smart as all of us."
—Eunice Parisi-Carew and Don Carew

Are You a Collaborative Leader?

These questions are from the UNITE model, as shown in Simple Truth #19 and taken from the book *Collaboration Begins with You: Be a Silo Buster* by Ken Blanchard, Jane Ripley, and Eunice Parisi-Carew. Circle Y (yes) or N (no) for each question.

Utilize Differences

1. Do I believe everyone has something to contribute?   Y / N
2. Do I ensure everyone in my group is heard?   Y / N
3. Do I actively seek different points of view?   Y / N
4. Do I encourage debate about ideas?   Y / N
5. Do I feel comfortable facilitating conflict?   Y / N

Nurture Safety and Trust

6. Do I encourage people to speak their mind?   Y / N
7. Do I consider all ideas before decisions are made?   Y / N
8. Do I share knowledge freely?   Y / N
9. Do I view mistakes as learning opportunities?   Y / N
10. Am I clear with others about what I expect?   Y / N

Involve Others in Crafting a Clear Purpose, Values, and Goals

11. Is my team committed to a shared purpose? Y / N
12. Do I know the purpose of our project and why it is important? Y / N
13. Do I hold myself and others accountable for adhering to our values? Y / N
14. Do I check decisions against our stated values? Y / N
15. Do I hold myself and others accountable for project outcomes? Y / N

Talk Openly

16. Do others consider me a good listener? Y / N
17. Do I share information about myself with my teammates? Y / N
18. Do I seek information and ask questions? Y / N
19. Do I give constructive feedback—and am I open to receiving feedback? Y / N
20. Do I encourage people to network with others? Y / N

Empower Yourself and Others

21. Do I continually work to develop my competence? Y / N
22. Do I feel empowered to give my opinions during idea sessions, even if I disagree? Y / N
23. Do I actively build and share my network with others? Y / N
24. Do I share my skills and knowledge with other departments? Y / N

25. Do I believe my work is important to the organization?   Y / N

Now give yourself one point for every Yes answer. What is your total score? _____

A score of 21 to 25 is outstanding! Keep up the good work!

A score of 17 to 20 is very good. You are definitely on the right track.

A score of 14 to 16 is average. Keep working on these skills.

A score of 13 or less is poor. Pay attention—there is lots of room for improvement!

Love is the answer.
What is the question?

Do You Lead with Love?

Take a look at these nine components of love, based on the thoughts of Henry Drummond. As you read, think about how you model these qualities in your leadership.

- You model love as *patience* when people aren't performing well, and you help them figure out the problem and rebuild their self-confidence.
- You model love as *kindness* when you take the time to smile and greet coworkers, share a loving thought with a family member, or help a stranger.
- You model love as *generosity* when you use your time, talent, or treasure to help people be the best they can be and rejoice over the successes of others.
- You model love as *courtesy* when you show up to meetings on time and are pleasant and helpful to others.
- You demonstrate love as *humility* when you credit your successes to the contributions of your team members and recognize that "no one of us is as smart as all of us."
- You demonstrate love as *unselfishness* when you make decisions based on the well-being of others and believe leadership is about serving, not being served.
- You demonstrate love as *good temper* when you make a choice to exhibit self-control if provoked by people or circumstances.

- You demonstrate love as *guilelessness* when you trust people instead of judging them, give them the benefit of the doubt, and assume good intentions.
- You demonstrate love as *sincerity* when you present your authentic self to the world, are forthright with others, mean what you say, and say what you mean.

Take a moment to self-reflect. As a leader, when do you demonstrate or struggle to demonstrate each of these qualities? Write about three areas that are your strengths and three that you need to improve.

_____

_____

_____

_____

_____

_____

_____

_____

_____

_____

_____

_____

_____

_____

_____

_____

_____

Building trust is a skill that can be learned and developed.

Are You a Trustworthy Leader?

Identify how often you engage in trustworthy behavior by using the ABCD model from Simple Truth #28. Use this rating scale: 1=almost never; 2=infrequently; 3=occasionally; 4=sometimes; 5=almost always; 6=always.

Able

1. Demonstrate strong task knowledge and skills. _____
2. Have a track record of achieving results. _____
3. Demonstrate strong problem-solving skills. _____

Total for Able _____

Believable

4. Tell the truth. _____
5. Act in alignment with personal and organizational values. _____
6. Avoid gossip and playing favorites. _____

Total for Believable _____

Connected

7. Care about others' well-being. _____
8. Take time to connect and converse. _____
9. Find common ground with others. _____

Total for Connected _____

Dependable

10. Consistently follow through on commitments. _____
11. Hold myself and others accountable. _____
12. Reply thoughtfully and quickly. _____

Total for Dependable _____

My highest scoring element of trust:
☐ Able   ☐ Believable   ☐ Connected   ☐ Dependable

My lowest scoring element of trust:
☐ Able   ☐ Believable   ☐ Connected   ☐ Dependable

My second-lowest scoring element of trust:
☐ Able   ☐ Believable   ☐ Connected   ☐ Dependable

Actions I will take to increase my trustworthiness:

_____

_____

_____

_____

"Self-trust is the first secret of success."—Ralph Waldo Emerson

Creating Your Leadership Point of View

Use the following steps to create an initial draft of your Leadership Point of View (LPOV). Take your time!

1. *Key people*—List the people in your life who impacted you the most. Answer these questions:

   a. Who mentored you? Taught you? Inspired you? Helped you believe in yourself?
   b. What did you admire (or not admire) about each of these people?
   c. What did you learn from each of these people that shaped your leader behavior?

2. *Key events*—Identify the events in your life that impacted you the most. Answer these questions:

   a. What events do you remember very clearly?
   b. What have been turning points in your life?
   c. What experiences in your past prepared you for a leadership role?
   d. What did you learn from each experience?

3. *Values*—What are your top three to five values when leading others? Values determine how you behave as a leader and are often shaped by the key people and events in our lives. Brainstorm the values that are important to you, and narrow them down to the three to five most critical. (See also Simple Truth #41.)

4. *Expectations for yourself and others*—Clarifying expectations for yourself and others is the last step in crafting your LPOV. These expectations should flow naturally from the people and key events that have influenced you and your values.

Combine these four sections into a written narrative. Share the draft of your LPOV with a confidant and get their feedback. Make additional changes, and schedule a time to share your LPOV with others.

A relationship with no trust is like a cell phone with no service or internet— all you can do is play games.

Be REAL: Reveal, Engage, Acknowledge, Listen

Show your authentic self by taking these four steps.

- Reveal information about yourself. Research shows that people want to have authentic relationships with their leaders. They want to know the person behind the title. Finish this sentence: This week I will help people learn more about me by _____

  _____

  _____

  _____

- Engage employees as individuals. Every employee wants to be seen and known as an individual, not just a number showing up to do a job. Get to know people individually by having regular 1:1 or small-group meetings, building rapport, and scheduling times to be together in person. Finish this sentence: This week I will engage _____ [name of person/team] by

  _____

  _____

- Acknowledge employee contributions. People are thirsty for acknowledgment of their contributions. Authentically acknowledging the work of your team members is a great way to build trust. Finish this sentence: This week I will acknowledge _____ [name of person/team] by _____

  _____

  _____

  _____

- Listen to learn. When you interact with employees, spend more time listening than talking. The simple act of listening signals to the other person that what they have to say is important and that you value what's being communicated. Finish this sentence: This week I will take time to listen to _____ [name of person/team] by _____

  _____

  _____

  _____

SIMPLE TRUTH #37:

"Your actions speak so loudly I cannot hear what you are saying."—Anonymous

Do You Lead with Integrity?

Rate yourself on these characteristics of integrity. Where do you score high? Where do you score low? What do you need to improve? How would others rate you? Use this scale: 1=almost never; 2=infrequently; 3=occasionally; 4=sometimes; 5=almost always; 6=always.

Honesty: I am truthful and straightforward in my dealings with others. _____

Consistency: My actions and words align, and I maintain the same principles in all situations. _____

Ethical behavior: I follow ethical principles and stand up for what is right, even in difficult circumstances. _____

Trustworthiness: I demonstrate competence, integrity, care, concern, and reliability in my interactions with others. _____

Responsibility: I take ownership of my actions and decisions and hold myself accountable for the consequences. _____

Respect for others: I treat others with dignity and respect, regardless of their background or circumstances. _____

Courage: I have the courage to do what is right, even when it is unpopular or difficult. _____

Total Score: _____

If you scored

37–42: You are a role model of integrity. Excellent!

33–36: You frequently demonstrate integrity in your actions. Well done!

29–32: You demonstrate a moderate amount of integrity in your actions.

Below 29: Dedicate time and effort to consistently act with integrity.

Works Cited

Blanchard, Ken, John P. Carlos, and Alan Randolph. *Empowerment Takes More Than a Minute*. San Francisco: Berrett-Koehler, 1996. (Simple Truth #12)

Blanchard, Ken, and Randy Conley. *Simple Truths of Leadership: 52 Ways to Be a Servant Leader and Build Trust*. Oakland: Berrett-Koehler, 2022. (Simple Truth #36)

Blanchard, Ken, et al. *Leading at a Higher Level: Blanchard on Leadership and Creating High Performing Organizations*. Upper Saddle River, NJ: FT Press, 2019. (Simple Truth #22 [chapter 14 with Pat Zigarmi and Judd Hoekstra])

Blanchard, Ken, and Spencer Johnson. *The One Minute Manager*. New York: HarperCollins, 2003, and *The New One Minute Manager*. New York: HarperCollins, 2015. (Simple Truth #4)

Blanchard, Ken, and Mark Miller. *The Secret: What Great Leaders Know and Do*. San Francisco: Berrett-Koehler, 2004. (Simple Truth #26)

Blanchard, Ken, Eunice Parisi-Carew, and Jane Ripley. *Collaboration Begins with You: Be a Silo Buster*. San Francisco: Berrett-Koehler, 2015. (Simple Truth #19)

Blanchard, Ken, and Jesse Stoner. *Full Steam Ahead! Unleash the Power of Vision in Your Work and Your Life*. San Francisco: Berrett-Koehler, 2003. (Simple Truth #2)

Blanchard, Ken, Patricia Zigarmi, and Drea Zigarmi. *Leadership and the One Minute Manager*. New York: Harper Collins, 2013. (Simple Truths #9, #10, and #18)

Drummond, Henry. *The Greatest Thing in the World and Other Addresses*. Chicago: Fleming H. Revell, 1898. (Simple Truth #20)

Acknowledgments

From Ken and Randy

We are thrilled to have Renee Broadwell join us on the cover of this playbook because of all the wonderful work she did to make it happen. We also want to thank our fabulous friends at Berrett-Koehler, especially Sarah Modlin and Edward Wade.

From Ken

I'm continuously thankful for my wife, Margie, and the lifetime of support I've received from her. And I'm always grateful for my wonderful teammates Martha Lawrence, Evelyn "Bibi" De La Garza, Vicki Stanford, and David Witt.

From Randy

I'm especially grateful for my wife, Kim, who is my lifetime "partner in trust." Special thanks go to Jason Weber (United States); Jayson Naidoo (South Africa); Piotr Karpowicz, Malgorzata Jakubicz, and the team at Blanchard Poland; and Stephanie Mo and Mike Lee (South Korea) for being global champions of *Simple Truths of Leadership*.

About the Authors

Ken Blanchard

One of the most influential leadership experts in the world, Ken Blanchard is coauthor of more than sixty-five books, including the iconic *The One Minute Manager*, with combined sales of over 23 million copies in forty-seven languages.

Ken is cofounder with his wife, Margie, of Blanchard (formerly The Ken Blanchard Companies), a globally recognized leadership training and consulting firm in San Diego, California. He also cofounded Lead Like Jesus, a worldwide organization committed to helping people become servant leaders.

Born in New Jersey and raised in New York, Ken received his master's degree from Colgate University and his bachelor's degree and doctorate from Cornell University.

Randy Conley

Randy Conley is vice president and trust practice leader for Blanchard. He is coauthor of Blanchard's Building Trust training program and works with organizations around the globe helping them build trust in the workplace.

Randy is coauthor of *Simple Truths of Leadership* with Ken Blanchard and a contributing author of *Leading at a Higher Level* with Ken Blanchard, *Trust, Inc.: Strategies for Building Your Company's Most Valuable Asset,* and *Trust, Inc.: 52 Weeks of Activities and Inspirations for Building Workplace Trust.* His award-winning *Leading with Trust* blog can be found at leadingwithtrust.com.

Randy holds a master of science degree in executive leadership from the University of San Diego. He and his wife, Kim, have two sons and reside in San Diego.

Renee Broadwell

Renee Broadwell is senior editor for Blanchard, where she has worked for sixteen years. She and Ken are coeditors of *Servant Leadership in Action: How You Can Achieve Great Relationships and Results.* She has served as lead editor on several of Ken's book projects, including *Simple Truths of Leadership, Legendary Service, Lead with LUV, Fit at Last, Collaboration Begins with You, The Simple Truths of Service,* and *Lead Like Jesus Revisited.*

Renee works with Blanchard's social media team as liaison with Ken on his personal LinkedIn page. She also writes and edits articles, blogs, and special projects for the marketing department and executive suite.

She and her husband, Grant, live in Escondido, California. Their grown children and fabulous granddaughter live nearby.

Connect with Blanchard®

For more than forty years, Blanchard® (formerly The Ken Blanchard Companies®) has been committed to creating inspired leaders through dynamic, human-powered learning experiences. Our solutions, including SLII®—the most widely used leadership training program in the world—are based on rigorous academic research and have been tested in thousands of workshops and refined to meet the needs of today's leaders.

To learn more, please connect with us at blanchard.com or

Blanchard Global Headquarters
125 State Place
Escondido, CA 92029
United States
+1.800.728.6000
+1.760.489.5005
blanchard.com

Join Ken and Randy Online

Ken Blanchard

Ken personally responds to your comments at linkedin.com/in/kenblanchard1.

For information on all of Ken's books, visit kenblanchardbooks.com.

Randy Conley

Website: randyconley.com

Randy's award-winning blog: leadingwithtrust.com

LinkedIn: linkedin.com/in/randy-conley

Twitter: @randyconley

NOTES

NOTES

NOTES

NOTES

NOTES

NOTES

NOTES

NOTES

NOTES

Dear reader,

Thank you for picking up this book and welcome to the worldwide BK community! You're joining a special group of people who have come together to create positive change in their lives, organizations, and communities.

What's BK all about?

Our mission is to connect people and ideas to create a world that works for all.

Why? Our communities, organizations, and lives get bogged down by old paradigms of self-interest, exclusion, hierarchy, and privilege. But we believe that can change. That's why we seek the leading experts on these challenges—and share their actionable ideas with you.

A welcome gift

To help you get started, we'd like to offer you a **free copy** of one of our bestselling ebooks:

www.bkconnection.com/welcome

When you claim your **free ebook**, you'll also be subscribed to our blog.

Our freshest insights

Access the best new tools and ideas for leaders at all levels on our blog at ideas.bkconnection.com.

Sincerely,

Your friends at Berrett-Koehler

Certified

Corporation